# MORE LIFE'S LITTLE
# FRUSTRATION BOOK

A Parody

By G. Gaynor McTigue

A Stonesong Press Book

# St. Martin's Paperbacks

MORE LIFE'S LITTLE FRUSTRATION BOOK

Copyright © 1997 by The Stonesong Press, Inc. and G. Gaynor McTigue.

ISBN: 0-312-96098-0

Printed in the United States of America

St. Martin's Paperbacks trade paperback edition/January 1997

10  9  8  7  6  5  4  3  2  1

# INTRODUCTION

When we last left you in *Life's Little Frustration Book*, something was preventing the refrigerator door from closing and you couldn't figure out what it was.

Still stumped? Well, you won't find the answer here. In fact, just when you thought you had those pesky little bugaboos of life licked (the refrigerator door notwithstanding), we present you with a fresh batch to irk you anew: *More Life's Little Frustration Book*.

But don't take these insidious aggravations too seriously. Remember, these are life's *little* frustrations. The ones we fortunately can cope with. The ones we hopefully can laugh at. Many thanks to my agent, Sheree Bykofsky, and Paul Fargis for their aggravating suggestions.

—G. Gaynor McTigue

Also by G. Gaynor McTigue

Life's Little Frustration Book
You Know You're Middle Aged When . . .
How *Not* to Make Love to a Woman


G. Gaynor McTigue can be reached for
questions and comment by E-mail at:
**jerrym321@aol.com**


Web site: **http://members.aol.com/jerrym321/books.htm**

1 ★ You drop your bread on the floor, butter side down.

2 ★ The label on your shirt collar is driving you crazy.

3 ★ The car in front you has its turn signal on . . . *thirteen straight miles.*

4 ★ You can't rip a window envelope in half.

5 ★ You wake up the entire household pulling a plastic cookie tray out of the wrapper.

6 ★ The toilet seat won't stay up on its own.

7 ★ The dirt smudge is *under* the Scotch tape.

8 ★ Your sinus-suffering blind date takes you out for fondue.

9 ★ You don't realize the milk is sour until you pour it on your $5-a-box cereal.

10 ★ Your new leather-soled shoes might as well be skates . . . and the sidewalk a rink.

11 ★ The insect crawling on your restaurant table *doesn't fly*.

12 ✶ The little foil pull tab on the orange juice carton is too short to pull.

13 ✶ "Some assembly required" turns out to be *The Lost Weekend.*

14 ✶ Deep in thought, you drop your Federal Express overnight letter in the mailbox.

**15** ★ You spend hundreds of dollars in a store whose cheap bags rip apart the minute you walk out.

**16** ★ Everything you have that's made of "space-age plastic" is scratched, broken, or discolored.

**17** ★ You forget to tip the skycap and your luggage winds up in Latvia.

18 ★ You bite hungrily into a blueberry muffin that turns out to be a moldy plain one.

19 ★ Your coat is always the one that ends up on the cloakroom floor.

20 ★ Plastic cafeteria trays are designed so that beverage bottles slide right off.

**21** ★ You lose half the needles on your $75 Christmas tree getting it through the door.

**22** ★ Just when you've got the layout of your supermarket all figured out, they rearrange the merchandise.

**23** ★ The portion you're supposed to detach and return with payment doesn't fit into its own envelope.

**24** ✶ Every time you use an airplane bathroom you hit turbulence.

**25** ✶ The washing instructions on your garment wash away.

26 ★ Your windshield wiper leaves a streak
right at eye level . . . Your windshield
wiper leaves a streak right at eye level
. . . Your windshield wiper leaves a streak
right at eye level . . .

27 ★ You get an itchy nose during a dental
procedure and can't do a damn thing
about it.

28 ✶ Horseflies are ingenious at getting into your house, but can never get out.

29 ✶ People leaving the movie theater reveal the ending as you're waiting in line.

30 ✶ Your spouse serves for dinner the same thing you had for lunch.

31 ★ Your body lotion erupts in your suitcase at 30,000 feet.

32 ★ You tear up a legitimate check thinking it's junk mail.

33 ★ You agree to a telephone survey and they keep rephrasing the same stupid questions over and over.

**34** ✶ It's finally your turn at the cash machine and the TEMPORARILY CLOSED FOR SERVICING sign flashes on.

**35** ✶ You max out on leftover Halloween candy.

**36** ✶ People who call up the store where you're waiting to be served . . . *get served first*.

**37** ∗ The waiter refills your half-empty cup of coffee, lousing up your perfect mixture of cream and sugar.

**38** ∗ You disembark from a harrowing four-hour plane ride and your cabbie drives like a maniac.

**39** ∗ Your Itty Bitty book light burns out during a climactic scene in the book.

**40** ★ The person walking past you on the train clobbers you in the head with her shoulder bag.

**41** ★ Tonight's the night you turn back the clock on your radio. And on your VCR . . . answering machine . . . microwave . . . fax . . . PC . . .

42 ★ Your fellow worshipers, so humble and contrite during church services, cut you off and curse you out in the parking lot.

43 ★ You thought life was complicated enough. Then came the Internet.

44 ★ Three weeks after subscribing to a magazine, you get your first renewal notice.

**45** ★ Your living room rug keeps curling up at one corner.

**46** ★ You keep tripping over it.

**47** ★ Your neighbor's dog slobbers all over you in the elevator.

**48** ★ You have to pretend you like it while pushing the mutt off.

**49** ✶ You pull open a file drawer and the entire cabinet crashes to the floor.

**50** ✶ Another family member quietly enters the room . . . asks you a question . . . and scares you half to death.

**51** ✶ You yearn for simpler days when the telephone company was a monopoly.

**52** ✶ The train everyone is waiting for on Track 7 is suddenly announced arriving on Track 2.

**53** ✶ You go out to select a wallpaper, thinking you'll be back in an hour.

**54** ✶ The driver of the bus you're standing on likes to create human waves.

**55** ∗ It occurs to you that if you're getting other people's mail, other people are getting yours.

**56** ∗ You're clueless how to dispose of the pizza box.

**57** ∗ Drivers without mufflers always do their cruising at 3 A.M.

**58** ✷ Your new bedside air conditioner leaves you cool . . . comfortable . . . and deaf in one ear.

**59** ✷ It kills you to throw away that last, embedded half-inch of deodorant stick.

**60** ✷ There's no place at the cocktail party to put your Swedish meatball toothpicks.

**61** ✳ You entertain the entire beach trying to set up a folding cabana chair.

**62** ✳ Your baby monitor intercepts a disparaging phone conversation . . . *about you.*

**63** ✳ The restaurant you take your client to reeks of latrine deodorizer.

**64** ★ The voice on a TV commercial is that of a famous actor and you can't figure out who it is.

**65** ★ Your checking account dips briefly below the minimum balance, and you get slapped with multiple exorbitant fees.

**66** ✶ That charming old house you bought last summer . . . clanks, hisses, and gurgles all winter.

**67** ✶ The face of the person you're talking to is much too close.

**68** ✶ Every time you back off, it leans closer.

**69** ★ You've got food stuck between your teeth and your tongue isn't the right tool for the job.

**70** ★ Your lunch mate laughingly associates your entrée with some kind of bodily function.

**71** ★ You finally get a chance to watch the hit TV show you only saw once, and it's the same episode.

**72** ★ You close the desk drawer and snap your ruler in half.

**73** ★ You can't pick up a magazine without getting prissy perfume scent all over you.

**74** ★ Just as the movie's starting, a six-foot-three punk with spiked hair sits in front of you.

**75** ✶ You bite into a bubbling hot serving of microwave lasagna . . . that's still frozen inside.

**76** ✶ The one day you get to rake the leaves, winds are gusting to 30 miles-per-hour.

**77** ✶ A year is just long enough to forget how you did something last year.

78 ✶ You want the window to stay up. It insists on sliding down. (The window wins.)

79 ✶ The tissues are wadded so tightly in the box, your first pull nets seven.

80 ✶ Just as you drink the last of your orange juice, you realize you forgot to take your vitamins.

**81** ✳ The fringes of your rug get sucked up into the vacuum cleaner.

**82** ✳ You have to plod through seven automated phone menus just to get a live voice.

**83** ✳ . . . which tells you you've got the wrong department.

**84** ★ Presidents' Day advertisers make George Washington and Abraham Lincoln look like complete idiots.

**85** ★ The paint that barely covers the wall takes forever to wash out of the brush.

**86** ★ Your nasty annual Christmas cold arrives right on schedule.

87 * The shopping bag keeps flopping over to one side.

88 * You stretch out your coiled telephone cord and pull the receiver off the table.

89 * The bread crust is separating from every slice in the loaf.

**90** ★ The guy in front of you at the newsstand is purchasing 25 lottery tickets.

**91** ★ The waiter joins in on your intimate conversation.

**92** ★ The book you're starting to read has a preface . . . *and* a forward . . . *and* an introduction.

**93** ★ For a brief terrifying instant, you think the elevator is free-falling.

**94** ★ You borrow an expensive power tool from a neighbor and it breaks while you're using it.

**95** ★ Even in this era of high technology, milk cartons still leak.

96 ★ You can't play a game of basketball without jamming a finger.

97 ★ It's your forecast from hell: "Snow mixing with or changing to sleet and freezing rain."

98 ★ As you're hurriedly writing down a phone message, the pencil point breaks.

**99** ✶ Two parts of the three-way bulb quickly burn out.

**100** ✶ You can't get workmen to show up for an estimate, much less a job.

**101** ✶ It takes you three hours to dig out your car . . . and three seconds for the snow-plow to bury it again.

**102** ✴ The size of the servings claimed on a food label couldn't satisfy a chipmunk.

**103** ✴ When you arrive at the ski resort, it's 55 degrees and pouring rain.

**104** ✴ No matter how you adjust them, your cheap sunglasses sit crookedly on your face.

**105** ★ You're still far back on the bathroom line when flashing lights signal that intermission is over.

**106** ★ "One size fits all" means it doesn't really fit anybody.

**107** ★ Someone always comes out of nowhere to beat you to the cash register.

**108** ✶ The red lights in the business district are perfectly timed so you hit every damn one of them.

**109** ✶ You flick your wrist to tear off the toilet paper and unravel about 15 feet.

**110** ✶ And can never roll it back up the way it was.

111 ∗ Lowlifes with loud mouths always sit behind you at baseball games.

112 ∗ You licked the stamp too much and now it won't stick.

113 ∗ Your stomach makes loud growling noises in the middle of a business meeting.

114 ★ You have to fumble around in the dark in a messy Portosan toilet.

115 ★ A year after writing a "thank you" note, you find it unmailed in your jacket pocket.

116 ★ Someone's been putting empty containers back into the refrigerator.

117 ★ The bread that's barely toasted when you check on it . . . is burnt just seconds later.

118 ★ Psychotherapists never tell you that you don't need to come anymore.

119 ★ When you talk to someone with mirrored sunglasses, you can't see what their eyes are saying and have to stare at your own reflection.

120 ★ That pile of unread magazines—and your guilt—is mounting.

121 ★ The many circular parts of table lamps are always coming loose.

122 ★ It's the third game of an 80-game season, and the announcers are billing it as a must-win situation for both teams.

123 ✳ You accidentally drop your toothbrush and it ricochets into the toilet.

124 ✳ . . . an unflushed toilet.

125 ✳ Just as you're passing a slow-moving car, it decides to speed up.

**126** ✶ You finally finish an agonizing hour-long game of Candy Land with your three-year-old . . . and she wants to play again.

**127** ✶ Your french fries taste like they've been cooked in machine oil.

**128** ✶ The pen in the post office never works . . . if it isn't missing in the first place.

129 ★ At a children's party, you bite into a cookie that's already been sucked on.

130 ★ Three dozen yellow jackets crash your outdoor barbecue.

131 ★ The plumber leaves a mess worse than what he had to fix.

132 ∗ Your straw slips irretrievably into the soda bottle.

133 ∗ You can't get those last few peas onto the fork without using your fingers.

134 ∗ You try cutting a cherry tomato in half and send it flying across the restaurant.

**135** ✶ Your enjoyment of soft, moist scrambled eggs is shattered by a crunchy piece of eggshell.

**136** ✶ There are some words your spell checker isn't very affective in detecting.

**137** ✶ One leaf always gets stuck in the rake.

**138** ★ Your car's windshield washer sprays over the roof.

**139** ★ You can't take notes on a little spiral notebook, because the friggin' little spiral is in the way.

**140** ★ You never loosen the laces enough to remove your boot on the first pull.

141 ★ You're stuck in traffic behind a big truck and have no idea what's happening up ahead.

142 ★ The busboy starts mopping the floor with ammonia while you're still eating.

143 ★ You put too much salt in the stew and there's no going back.

**144** ✶ The laser-printed characters on your letter flake off at the fold marks.

**145** ✶ You open your camera to remove the film
and discover you forgot to rewind it.

**146** ✶ The instructions for the foreign-made
product were written by someone with a
second-grade command of English.

**147** ★ It's not a matter of *if* the elastic band on your party hat will break, but *when*.

**148** ★ Could your swim goggles make you look any dorkier?

**149** ★ You blow out a flip-flop with a quarter mile of hot asphalt left to walk.

150 ★ You wish someone would please explain what measurements like degree days, statute miles, and knots mean.

151 ★ The flap pockets on your sport jacket are fake.

152 ★ If only you could get that last tasty piece of shrimp tail out of the shell.

**153** ✶ You forget to turn off the TV during a blackout and nearly jump out of your skin at 3 A.M. when the power comes back on.

**154** ✶ You discover that the back windows of your new car don't roll down.

**155** ✶ People keep filing past you saying "Excuse me" in a narrow library aisle.

**156** ⋆ You have cold hands from late October through early May.

**157** ⋆ Jokes directed at decaf drinkers are beginning to wear thin.

**158** ⋆ You ask if you can hold someone else's baby and it spits up all over you.

**159** ★ You get into a major traffic jam on a rural country back road during leaf season.

**160** ★ Every time you open your overstuffed closet, something falls on your head.

**161** ★ Candles always sit precariously in candlestick holders.

162 ★ The sweating iced tea glass drips all over your lap.

163 ★ They don't tell you in the TV listing that a show will be interrupted three times for a pledge drive.

164 ★ You unwittingly load dirty dishes into a dishwasher full of clean ones.

**165** ★ Precocious kids say nauseatingly adult things in TV commercials.

**166** ★ That bountiful bowl of fruit on your kitchen counter looks great, but at some point you've got to eat the stuff.

**167** ★ Nothing gnaws at your conscience like overdue library books.

168 ★ They discuss things like light days and heavy days in tampon TV commercials.

169 ★ Your name sticker keeps curling up and falling off your lapel.

170 ★ Everyone else's is doing just fine.

171 ★ You break a fingernail in an attempt to become a human staple remover.

172 ★ Tired, bloodshot, and disheveled after a long international flight, you enter a terminal to the stares of hundreds of people.

173 ★ You're roped in by an ad for an "estate sale," only to find a worthless collection of household junk.

174 ★ You have to run the water three minutes before the hot comes up.

175 ★ Your wool slacks keep sliding off the plastic hanger.

176 ★ Pedestrians foolishly insist on walking two abreast on narrow country roads.

177 ★ You live on a street with an embarrassing name like Lovers Lane or Old Sow Road.

178 ✶ You reach into a bush to retrieve a ball. A thorny bush.

179 ✶ You never know if the "Push here to cross" button made any difference.

180 ✶ You hope the fashionable name you give your baby this year isn't a played-out joke a decade from now.

181 ★ The ice cream cup is frozen solid, and they give you this useless little wooden stick to eat it with.

182 ★ It's one of those days where nothing you do is going to please you.

183 ★ You make your tie and it's a little too long. You make it again and it's a little too short. You make it again . . .

**184** ✶ You wonder how the gasoline industry duped you into pumping your own gas and washing your own windshield.

**185** ✶ Great. You just received another scratchy wool sweater you'll never wear.

**186** ✶ The unit price of the larger size is greater than the unit price of the smaller size.

187 ★ Rather than dry off in the shower, people drip all over the locker room floor.

188 ★ You're sick of cute little gift shops with dried flowers, calico pin cushions, and $10 jars of jam.

189 ★ Somewhere in the house you have an orphan glove, a pen without a cap, and sunglasses with a missing hinge screw.

**190** ✳ You don't remember those delicious leftovers until they've spoiled.

**191** ✳ Your next-door neighbor's kid takes up the drums.

**192** ✳ It's a given you'll mangle your finger either opening the beach umbrella or closing it.

**193** ✳ You launder your money. Literally.

**194** ★ You arrive at a charming inn for a romantic weekend and your room has two single beds.

**195** ★ Your sheet of postage stamps has an annoying little perforated fringe around the edge.

**196** ★ Someone comes up and says hello at a party and you can't remember who it is.

**197** ✶ Now you're expected to introduce the person to your spouse.

**198** ✶ You go to the store to pick up a single item, get distracted by other things you need, and forget what you originally came in for.

**199** ✶ The person walking in front of you on a dark street thinks you're going to mug her.

**200** ✳ Your kitchen cabinet is cluttered with extra packets of duck sauce you're never going to use.

**201** ✳ You feel like a suspect when walking past a store security guard without having bought anything.

202 ★ The recorded voice on the other end sounds so real, you stupidly start talking to it.

203 ★ You always get the clerk, waiter, or salesperson who's struggling through his first day on the job.

204 ✳ You're cornered at a party by someone with complex philosophical theories that make not a bit of sense.

205 ✳ Your home heating system creates an ideal indoor environment. For cacti.

206 ✳ You unwittingly wear a bright orange sweater on St. Patrick's Day.

**207** * Your morning paper never has last night's scores.

**208** * You discover that "bonded leather" isn't really leather.

**209** * The orange juice carton is too full to shake, so the first glass is pale and tasteless . . .

**210** * . . . and the rest is too sweet.

**211** ✶ No matter how well you think you've cut the sandwich, there's a part that's still connected.

**212** ✶ The only person you find to ask directions of says, "This is my first time here, too."

**213** ★ Your penis pops out between your underwear and your pants, and you pray your fly isn't open.

**214** ★ Now you have to reach into your pocket and maneuver it back in without looking like a pervert.

**215** ★ You tell an acquaintance you didn't know she was pregnant, and she says: "I'm not."

**216** ✶ The gauze pad has become part of the scab, and now it's time to come off.

**217** ✶ You hit a tremendous drive straight down the center of the fairway . . . and can't find it.

**218** ✶ You hit a tremendous drive straight down the center of the fairway . . . and dribble your next shot 15 feet.

**219** ∗ The waiter fails to inform you the plate is hot.

**220** ∗ Your guest brings a six-pack of beer . . . and heads straight for the twelve-year-old scotch.

**221** ∗ You nibble on your numbed lip after leaving the dentist, giving yourself a whopping cold sore later on.

**222** ★ People use the word opinionated to mean erudite or well-read.

**223** ★ Another shopper leaves his cart perfectly positioned in the supermarket aisle so you can't pass.

**224** ★ Then glares at you when you move it.

**225** ✶ Someone running the vacuum cleaner in another apartment is lousing up your TV reception.

**226** ✶ The base of your wine glass gets caught under your place mat, and you pour the contents into your lap.

**227** ✶ You have to blow up a whole bag of short-necked balloons.

**228** ✶ You nearly pass out in the process.

**229** ★ A gorgeous-looking person of the opposite sex smiles warmly, then says, "Oh, I'm sorry. I thought you were someone else."

**230** ★ "Ice" signs always have icicles depicted on them . . . like you don't get it.

**231** ★ Talk show radio hosts hang up on callers who disagree with them.

**232** * The auto mechanic always finds a couple of other things that need fixing, too.

**233** * Your peeler can't handle those little ravines in the potato.

**234** * You're at the ATM . . . you need cash . . . three people are waiting behind you . . . and you can't remember your PIN number.

**235** ✶ If the restaurant kitchen is anything like the restaurant bathroom . . .

**236** ✶ Whenever you really need a flashlight, there's only a minute of battery life left.

**237** ✶ The store brand sucks.

**238** ✶ Your neighbor installs a flashing neon Santa directly opposite your bedroom window.

**239** ✶ You're discreetly purchasing condoms at a drugstore and the clerk yells, "Hey, Joe, I need a price on the Trojan Magnums!"

**240** ✶ No software you ever bought did anything with "just a click."

**241** ★ You send out 50 invitations to a party you scheduled for September 31.

**242** ★ While traveling overseas, you see your fellow countrymen making complete asses of themselves.

**243** ★ Your new, slick-looking sneaker laces can't even hold a knot.

**244** ✴ The recording says, "The number you have dialed is no longer in service" . . . but never tells you why.

**245** ✴ The contractor's discount coupon must be submitted *before* he gives you an estimate.

**246** ✴ Doctors have a new way to make you wait: They shuffle you from room to room so you think you're getting somewhere.

**247** ★ During a bout of diarrhea, you get the bathroom stall next to your boss.

**248** ★ Appliance repair shops charge you $40–50 for an estimate, virtually ensuring you'll have to accept it.

**249** ★ Your neighbor dry-docks his 20-foot cabin cruiser in the driveway next to your house.

**250** ★ You laugh during a play when nobody else does, and realize it wasn't supposed to be funny.

**251** ★ The conductor has to shout "Tickets!" three times before you wake up.

**252** ★ The Life Savers are stuck together and you can't get them apart.

**253** ★ Count on your dependable local post office to be out of what you need. Again.

**254** ★ You burst in on someone who didn't lock the bathroom door.

**255** ★ You've reached the age where you need a digital rectal exam *every year*.

**256** ✶ The morning paper always lands on the passenger side of the driveway.

**257** ✶ Sports announcers are forever denouncing hockey fights, but it's the first thing they show when the highlights come on.

**258** ✶ Sitcoms add hilarious laugh tracks to things that aren't even funny.

**259** * You're so conditioned to using a calculator, you can't do simple arithmetic anymore.

**260** * If the studio audiences of trashy talk shows are so disgusted with the guests, what are they doing there in the first place?

**261** ✴ You can't separate the shopping cart from the pack.

**262** ✴ Graduation caps were designed to make your graduation pictures look stupid.

**263** ✴ Some people always answer "What?" even when they've heard what you said.

**264** ★ News reports of government rip-offs always try to rile you by saying "and you're paying for it!"

**265** ★ You get into a pleasant conversation with someone in the supermarket and the person suddenly asks, "Do you love Jesus?"

**266** ★ The monument you traveled halfway around the world to see is in scaffolding.

**267** ✶ You fail to notice the split level and stumble into a living room full of people.

**268** ✶ They tell you inflation went up 5%, but if you factor out food, energy, and housing costs, it didn't go up at all.

**269** ✶ The crucial paragraph of text at the start of the movie fades away before you're half-finished.

270 ★ A store puts previously used or damaged merchandise back on the shelf.

271 ★ You crack a joke the same time someone else does and don't know which one they're laughing at.

272 ★ A TV station broadcasts 30 seconds of dead air where a commercial was supposed to be.

273 ★ The locker room bench is just the right width so that everything you put on it falls off.

274 ★ People who buy shoreline property expect the government to stem the inexorable advance of the ocean.

**275** ✶ You mistakenly dial someone's fax line and get an ear-piercing beep for your trouble.

**276** ✶ Your modem reaches someone's regular phone line, and you hear a tiny voice in your computer saying, "Hello, hello!"

**277** ✶ You scratch the lens of your new sun-glasses trying to get those stupid stickers off.

**278** ✶ Your neighbor's dog routinely fertilizes your lawn.

**279** ✶ The movies on your "premium" cable TV channel are getting lousier and lousier.

**280** ★ A store advertises: "We're extending this fabulous sale!" . . . because they can't get rid of the junk.

**281** ★ Your felt-tip pen makes lousy carbon copies.

**282** ★ Three weeks always pass between the time you lose a sock in the laundry and the day you find it.

**283** ★ You nearly die when the parking lot attendant comes screeching down the curved ramp in your brand-new car.

**284** ★ You have roaches, because your slobbo neighbor has roaches.

**285** ★ Ignoring the coasters, your guests put their highball glasses on your antique furniture.

**286** ✶ You can't get too chummy with anyone at a Halloween party, because you don't know what they really look like.

**287** ✶ People in front of you on the checkout line keep going back for more groceries.

**288** ✶ . . . and because they're not back in time, *you* have to start unloading their cart.

**289** ⋆ You have to keep coming up with block-buster ideas for your kids' birthday parties.

**290** ⋆ Products tell you to "apply liberally," so you'll need more sooner.

**291** ⋆ You never know who should go first at a four-way stop sign, because nobody comes to a full stop.

**292** ★ Millions of self-help books are sold each year, but you're not seeing any results.

**293** ★ You turn on the radio in the middle of an emergency test and think it's for real.

**294** ★ The table napkins got mixed up between dinner and dessert, and you can't tell which one is yours.

**295** ★ Your luggage comes around the baggage carousel opened, showcasing your underwear.

**296** ★ Your toilet ticks.

**297** ★ You send away for more information about an investment opportunity and a smarmy sales rep hounds you day and night.

**298** ★ Your dog licks his private parts in a room full of guests.

**299** ★ You're awakened by a phone call, then have to find a clear, cheery voice to say: "No, I've been up for hours."

**300** ★ The discount dining club you joined features mostly restaurants that are on the skids.

**301** ★ You have to exit a dark movie theater into bright sunshine.

**302** ★ You spend two weeks shelling out 15–20% gratuities in a foreign country where tipping isn't required.

**303** ★ Anyone who's ever transferred a business call for you has said, "I'm not quite sure how to do this" . . . and then cut you off.

**304** ✶ You shake a bottle of salad dressing whose cap is sitting loosely on its neck.

**305** ✶ You fill a cart with groceries, arrive at the checkout, then realize you don't have any money with you.

**306** ✶ A friend keeps boring you with lengthy descriptions of her epic dreams.

**307** ✶ You bought your house at peak.

**308** ✶ People stuff used tissues in your car ashtray.

**309** ✶ Clumps of cocoa float undissolved at the top of your mug.

**310** ★ The house painter appropriates the use of your front lawn for his billboard advertising.

**311** ★ White-collar executives strew their coffee cups, newspapers, and other garbage all over the train.

**312** ✶ You pay exorbitant prices to attend sporting events in which millionaire athletes give lackluster performances.

**313** ✶ Your crab cakes smell like low tide.

**314** ✶ Convicted politicians not only have the audacity to run again . . . they get re-elected.

**315** ✶ Survey questionnaires of political action committees are ridiculously biased in their favor.

**316** ✶ Coffee shops invariably forget your beverage when you ask for just water.

**317** ✶ Computer hardware and software companies have you on an upgrade treadmill.

**318** * Just when you pass a parked car in a lot, its reverse lights go on and the car behind you gets the space.

**319** * You're bombarded by fragrance commercials that make you feel sexually inadequate.

**320** * You have to interrupt good dinner conversation to go to the salad bar.

**321** ★ Parents wouldn't dare let small children create a ruckus in a movie theater, but think nothing of letting them disrupt church services.

**322** ★ No matter where you go, hotel rooms have the same layout, furnishings, and stale smell.

**323** * Children's movies are two-hour commercials for new toys your kids will be hounding you to get.

**324** * People set their fax machines to answer after three rings (like you have to give it time to get to the phone).

**325** * Someone in your group at the restaurant gets loud and obnoxious.

**326** ✶ You have to make small talk with the baby-sitter while driving her home at 1 A.M.

**327** ✶ The coach of your local pro team keeps puzzling over its lousy performance, when obviously the problem is him.

**328** ✳ You have to listen to dull presentation speeches by lifeless sponsor executives after TV golf tournaments.

**329** ✳ Every sport you play requires a different, and expensive, pair of shoes.

**330** ✳ You have to eat birthday cake that some kid, blowing out the candles, just sprayed his germs all over.

**331** ✶ Someone comes in at the end of your long story and asks, "What was that?"

**332** ✶ A guest takes your seat at the head of the table.

**333** ✶ You park your car beneath a tree that drips sap all over it.

**334** ★ You have leftover food that's too little to save . . . but enough to make you think it's a sin to throw away.

**335** ★ People who haven't found a reason to go to the library in 30 years . . . think the Internet is going to change their lives.

**336** ★ Of different political persuasions, you and your spouse cancel out each other's vote.

**337** ⋆ You show up at a party dressed to the nines and everyone else is in jeans.

**338** ⋆ Your vitamins make you pee a curious yellow.

**339** ⋆ Celebrities who are being paid fortunes to endorse products have to read dummy cards during 30-second commercials.

340 ★ Most poetry doesn't make any sense to you.

341 ★ Your spectacular high-rise view of the city is obliterated by another new high-rise.

342 ★ At the worst stage of your cold, you're asked to give a talk.

**343** ✶ The plane you were supposed to leave on an hour ago hasn't even arrived at the airport yet.

**344** ✶ There's an expensive article of clothing in your closet that you've never worn, and you rue the day you bought it.

**345** ★ Ads in hard-core industrial magazines use women in bikinis to present machine parts.

**346** ★ They always give the sports scores too fast.

**347** ★ You have to wish someone a generic "Happy holiday" because you don't know what their religion is.

**348** ✶ You throw out your lower back and nearly hit the roof when you sneeze.

**349** ✶ You have to decide which of the 25 different varieties of bakery cookies will comprise your pound.

**350** ✶ The doctor you thought stopped by your hospital bed to say hello charges you $200 for the visit.

**351** * The night nurse wakes you up to give you a sleeping pill.

**352** * Your hospital gown is like the great Continental Divide in the back.

**353** * The fast song you're dancing to has a beat you can't figure out.

**354** * A flying cicada crashes into your head.

**355** ∗ The newspaper refers to criminals, terrorists, and other social deviants as "Mr."

**356** ∗ Your dinner host's dog keeps nudging you under the table for scraps.

**357** ∗ You fart audibly and have to cover it up with a quick burst of conversation.

**358** ★ You realize that fast-food restaurants aren't as cheap as they're made out to be.

**359** ★ You prick your finger 14 times decking the halls with boughs of holly.

**360** ★ If you bought everything advertisers insist you need, you'd have to be Bill Gates.

**361** ★ You swallow a mouthful of murky pool water.

**362** ★ There's always one joker on the plane who insists on keeping his window shade open during the movie.

**363** ★ You're awakened at 5 A.M. every morning by the same two screeching crows.

**364** ★ All the kitty litter in the world won't disguise the fact that your cat poops.

**365** ★ The postcard for a "private sale" is addressed to you or "current resident."

**366** ★ The cover of the original *Life's Little Frustration Book* promises "365 ignominious aggravations," when there are only 364. (Now we're even.)